Ketogenic Instant pot & Ketogenic delicious recipes

Author : Megan Walther and James soul

Ketogenic Instant Pot Cookbook

Make Yummy Ketogenic Diet Meals With Instant Pot

Table of Contents

Introduction

I am so glad you took time out of your busy schedule to download your copy of *Ketogenic Instant Pot Cookbook: Make Yummy Ketogenic Diet Meals with Instant Pot*. Thank you for doing so. The following chapters will discuss some of the many different ways you can stay on your keto diet plan with the aid of your Instant Pot.

The plan goes by many different names such as the low-carb diet, keto diet, and the low-carbohydrate diet & high-fat (LCHF) diet plan. Your liver produces ketones that are used as energy to provide adequate levels of proteins similar to other low-carbohydrate diet techniques. The process known as ketosis is natural and happens every day—no matter the total of carbs consumed.

There are plenty of books on this subject on the market, thanks again for choosing this one! Every effort was made to ensure it is full of as much useful information as possible. Please enjoy each of the recipes with the nutritional values listed including calories, protein, fat, and net carbohydrates (carbs).

Let's Begin!

Chapter 1: Delicious Breakfast Choices

Try one of these tasty dishes when you want a healthy start to your day.

Almond–Chia & Coconut Pudding

Prep & Cook Time: 20 min.

Yields: 4 Servings
Nutrition Values: Calories: 130 | Fat: 12 g | Protein: 14 g |Net Carbs: 1.5 g

Ingredients:

¼ c. shredded coconut
½ c. of each:

- Chopped almonds
- Chia seeds

2 c. almond milk

Preparation Method:

1. Measure out all of the fixings and add to the Instant Pot, stirring well.
2. Secure the lid and select the high setting (2-5 minutes) Quick release the pressure and place the pudding into four serving glasses.

Deviled Egg Salad

Prep & Cook Time: 30 min.

Yields: 5 Servings
Nutrition Values: Calories: 313 | Fat: 26.4 g | Protein: 16.4 g | Net Carbs: 1.3 g

Ingredients:

5 raw bacon strips

10 large eggs

2 tbsp. mayo

1 t. Dijon mustard

1 stalk green onion

¼ t. smoked paprika

Pepper & Salt to taste

Also Needed: 6-7-inch cake pan

Preparation Method:

1. Grease all sides of the pan that will sit inside of the pot on the trivet. Pour one cup of cold water in the bottom of the Instant Pot and add the steam rack.
2. Crack the eggs open in the pan (try not to break the yolks).

3. Place the pan on the rack. Secure the lid and set the timer for 6 minutes (high-pressure). Natural release the pressure and remove the pan.
4. Dab away any moisture. Flip the pan on a cutting board for the egg loaf to release. Chop and add to a mixing dish.
5. Clean the Instant Pot bowl and choose the sauté function (medium heat). Prepare the bacon until crispy.
6. Add to the chopped eggs with the mustard, mayo, paprika, pepper, and salt. Toss and garnish with green onion.
7. Serve the way you like it!

Egg Cups & Cheese

Prep & Cook Time: 15 min.

Yields: 4 Servings
Nutrition Values: Calories: 115 | Fat: 9 g | Protein: 9 g | Net Carbs: 2 g

Ingredients:

4 eggs

½ c. sharp shredded cheddar cheese

1 c. diced veggies—example, tomatoes, mushrooms, etc.

¼ c. Half & Half

Pepper & Salt to taste

2 tbsp. cilantro—chopped

Ingredients for the Topping:

½ c. shredded cheese your choice

Also Needed:

- 4 wide-mouthed jars
- 2 c. water

Preparation Method:

1. Whisk the veggies, eggs, Half & Half, salt, pepper, cheese, and cilantro.
2. Combine the mixture into each of the jars. Secure the lids (not too tight) to keep water from getting into the egg mix.
3. Arrange the trivet in the Instant Pot and add the water. Arrange the jars on the trivet and set the timer for 5 minutes (high pressure). When done, quick release the pressure, and top with the rest of the cheese (½ cup).
4. Broil if you like for 2-3 minutes until the cheese is browned to your liking.

Ketogenic Eggs

Prep & Cook Time: 20 min.

Yields: 4 Servings
Nutrition Values: Fat: 14.4 g | Protein: 7.3 g | Net Carbs: 8.3 g

Ingredients:

1 tbsp. chopped shallot

3 tbsp. ghee

1 sliced jalapeno—matchstick

1 t. of each:

- Ground cinnamon
- Cumin seeds

3 sliced garlic cloves

1 coarsely chopped green bell pepper

2 coarsely chopped tomatoes

½ t. of each:

- Turmeric
- Ground ginger
- Salt

½ c. chopped cilantro

4 eggs—beaten

Preparation Method:

1. Add the ghee to the Instant Pot. Melt using the sauté function and add the cumin seeds, cooking until aromatic.

2. Continue cooking for 3 minutes along with the shallots. Stir in the peppers, tomatoes, jalapenos, and garlic. Sauté 3 additional minutes and add the salt, ginger, salt, and turmeric.

3. Whisk in the eggs and cook until set (30 seconds). When the eggs are at the right texture, sprinkle with the pepper, salt, and cilantro.

4. Secure the lid and prepare for 13 minutes. Quick release the steam and serve.

Paprika Boiled Eggs

Prep & Cook Time: 30 min.

Yields: 3 Servings
Nutrition Values: Calories: 72 | Fat: 5 g | Protein: 6.3 g | Net Carbs: 0.4 g

Ingredients:

6-8 eggs (from the fridge is okay)
1 c. cold water
Paprika

Preparation Method:

1. Add the water to the Instant Pot stainless bowl and add the steamer basket. Gently place the eggs and close the lid.

2. Set the timer for 5-10 minutes. Quick release and remove the eggs. When done, place in an ice-cold bath to cool, and peel.

3. Arrange the eggs on a serving platter and sprinkle with the paprika.

Sausage Cheese Ring

Prep & Cook Time: 50 min.

Yields: 4-6 Servings
Nutrition Values: Calories: 470 | Fat: 35.9 g | Protein: 28.5 g | Net Carbs: 3.6 g

Ingredients:

2 ½ tbsp. coconut oil
2 red bell peppers—½-inch cut
1 lb. breakfast sausage
4 large eggs
Ground pepper and salt—to taste
4 ½ tbsp. shredded parmesan cheese

Preparation Method:

1. Warm up the coconut oil in the Instant Pot and add the pepper pieces.
2. Slice the sausages into ringlets and sauté 2-5 minutes. Set aside.
3. Add 4 pepper ringlets in the pot. Add the egg to a dish and slide it into the center of the pepper ring. Give it a shake of pepper and salt. Do this with each one. Place the sausages on top (10-15 minutes).
4. Remove the rings and serve with the cheese topping.

Chapter 2: Luncheon Dishes

Lunchtime Cauliflower Soufflé

Prep & Cook Time: 32 min.

Yields: 6 Servings
Nutrition Values: Calories: 342 | Fat: 28 g | Protein: 17 g | Net Carbs: 5 g

Ingredients:

2 eggs
1 head cauliflower
½ c. of each:

- Asiago cheese
- Sour cream/Yogurt

2 tbsp. cream
2 oz. cream cheese
1 c. mild/sharp cheddar cheese
2 t. softened butter/ghee
¼ c. chives
Optional: 6 slices crumbled cooked bacon

Preparation Method:

1. Combine the two kinds of cheese, sour cream, cream cheese, cream, and eggs in a food processor. Pulse until smooth and frothy.
2. Chop the cauliflower and add to the mixture (pulse 2 seconds at a time). Blend in the butter and chives. Empty into a 1 ¼-quart casserole dish.
3. Pour the water into the Instant Pot. Secure the top and cook for 12 minutes using the high-pressure setting.

Natural release for 10 minutes, and quick release.

4. Garnish with the bacon if you choose.

Soups

Cabbage Roll "Unstuffed" Soup

Prep & Cook Time: 41 min.

Yields: 9 Servings
Nutrition Values: Calories: 217 | Fat: 14.8 g | Protein: 15.6 g | Net Carbs: 4.3 g

Ingredients:

2 minced garlic cloves

½ small diced onion

1 ½ lb. ground beef—80/20

¼ c. Bragg's Aminos

1 can (8oz.) tomato sauce

3 c. beef broth

3 t. Worcestershire sauce "keto" approved/another substitute

1 can diced tomatoes (14 oz.)

1 med. chopped cabbage

½ t. of each:

- Pepper

- Parsley
- Salt

Preparation Method:

1. Prepare using the sauté function on the Instant pot to brown the beef, garlic, and onions. Drain and add back to the pot with the rest of the fixings.
2. Program the unit on the soup function. Natural release the soup for about 10 minutes, and quick release the rest of the steam. Stir and serve.

Chicken Curry Soup

Prep & Cook Time: 36 mins.

Yields: 6 Servings
Nutrition Values: 108 Calories | Fat: 4 g | Protein: 15 g | Net Carbs: 3 g

Ingredients:

1 ½ c. unsweetened coconut milk
1 lb. chicken thighs—no skin
3-4 crushed garlic cloves
½ finely diced onion
2-inch knob ginger—minced
1 c. sliced mushrooms
4 oz. baby spinach
½ t. of each:

- Cayenne pepper
- Turmeric

1 t. of each:

- Salt
- Garam masala

¼ c. chopped cilantro

Preparation Method:

1. Combine all of the fixings in the Instant Pot. Set the high pressure for 10 minutes. Natural release the pressure when the cycle is completed.
2. Remove and shred the thighs. Add the meat to the pot.
3. Stir the juices and meat for a minute or so. Serve and enjoy!

Chicken Mushroom Soup

Prep & Cook Time: 31 min.

Yields: 4 Servings
Nutrition Values: Calories: 289 | Fat: 15 g | Protein: 30 g | Net Carbs: 9 g

Ingredients:

3 minced garlic cloves
1 thinly sliced onion
1 chopped yellow squash
2 c. mushrooms—chopped
1 lb. chicken breasts—remove bones and skin
2 ½ c. chicken stock
Pepper & Salt
1 t. Poultry/Italian Seasoning

Optional: ½ c. heavy whipping cream

Preparation Method:

1. Toss everything into the Instant Pot and cook for 15 minutes under high pressure. Natural release for 10 minutes; then quick release.
2. Remove the chicken and roughly puree the veggies with an immersion blender.
3. Shred the chicken and add it back to the cooker.
4. Add the cream, stir, and serve.

Ham & Beans

Prep & Cook Time: 1 hr. 8 min.

Yields: 6 Servings
Nutrition Values: Calories: 269| Fat: 14 g | Protein: 21 g | Net Carbs: 13 g

Ingredients:

1 c. of each:

- Chopped onion
- Dried black soybeans—after soaking yields = 2 c. beans
- Chopped celery

1 t. of each:

- Dried oregano
- Cajun seasoning
- Salt—maybe ½ t.
- Liquid smoke
- Louisiana Hot Sauce

4 minced garlic cloves
2 t. all-purpose seasoning
2 smoked ham hocks
2 c. of each:

- Water
- Chopped ham

Preparation Method:

1. Add all of the fixings to your Instant Pot and choose the bean/chili function (30 minutes, high-pressure). Natural release for 10 minutes, and quick release the rest of the pressure.

2. Trash the bone and add the meat back in the soup. Roughly puree some of the soup with an immersion blender.

3. Enjoy piping hot with some hot sauce on the side.

Jalapeno Popper Soup

Prep & Cook Time: 52 min.

Yields: 8 Servings
Nutrition Values: Calories: 571 | Fat: 40.1 g | Protein: 41.2 g | Net Carbs: 2.1 g

Ingredients:

½ lb. bacon—cooked and crumbled
1 ½ lb. chicken breasts (boneless skinless)
½ c. heavy whipping cream
3 tbsp. butter
½ chopped onion
2 minced garlic cloves
½ chopped green pepper
2 jalapenos—seeded and chopped
6 oz. cream cheese
3 c. chicken broth
½ t. pepper
1 t. of each:

- Salt
- Cumin

¼ t. paprika
½ t. xanthan gum
¾ c. of each cheese:

- Cheddar
- Monterrey Jack

Preparation Method:

1. Prepare the Instant Pot using the sauté function. Add the onions, butter, jalapenos, green peppers, and the

seasoning. Sauté until translucent. Stir in the cubed chicken, broth, and cream cheese.

2. Set the timer for 15 minutes—manual. Allow for 5 minutes natural release. Quick release after that time.
3. Choose the sauté function and remove the chicken from the bone using two forks. Add the chicken, whipping cream, both kinds of cheese, and the cooked bacon. Sprinkle the xanthan gum to thicken the soup.
4. Simmer for a few minutes and serve with some grated cheese, jalapenos, or bacon on the top.

Chilies & Stews

Chicken Stew

Prep & Cook Time: 50 min.

Yields: 8 Servings
Nutrition Values: Calories: 290| Fat: 37 g | Protein: 27 g | Net Carbs: 3 g

Ingredients:

2 lb. cut-up chicken
2 diced celery stalks
3 diced carrots
1 diced onion
2 bay leaves
Fresh herbs to taste—sage, rosemary, or basil
8-12 c. liquid—broth or water

Preparation Method:

1. Use the sauté function on the Instant Pot to prepare the celery, onions, and carrots until aromatic.
2. Toss in the rest of the ingredients and secure the lid.
3. Cook for 35 minutes using the high-pressure setting.
4. Natural release the pressure and serve.

Lamb Stew

Prep & Cook Time: 50 min.

Yields: 6 Servings
Nutrition Values: Calories: 300 | Fat: 15 g | Protein: 16 g | Net Carbs: 15 g

Ingredients:

1 acorn squash diced into cubes
2 lb. lamb
1 diced onion
3 diced carrots
1 bay leaf
1 large rosemary sprig/1 tbsp. dried
6 minced garlic cloves
3 tbsp. broth—any flavor

Preparation Method:

1. Sauté the onions and carrots using the sauté function in the Instant Pot. Blend in the lamb and brown slightly.

2. Toss in the rest of the fixings and prepare under high pressure (lid closed) for 35 minutes.

3. Natural release the pressure and enjoy.

No-Beans Beef Chili

Prep & Cook Time: 30 min.

Yields: 8 Servings
Nutrition Values: Calories: 326 | Fat: 17 g | Protein: 23 g | Net Carbs: 8 g

Ingredients:

2 lbs. beef
2 cans tomato sauce—15 oz. each
1 t. of each:

- Tabasco sauce
- Garlic powder/ 2 minced cloves
- Powdered/Dried oregano

1 can tomato paste—6 oz.
2 tbsp. cumin powder
5 tbsp. chili powder
½ c. dried onion flakes/ 1 med. onion chopped
2 t. fine ground sea salt
For Thinning: 1 c. chicken/beef broth

Preparation Method:

1. Finely chop the onion. Use the sauté function in the Instant Pot to brown the hamburger. Blend in the Tabasco, garlic, or onion flakes, cumin, salt, chili powder, and oregano. Mix thoroughly.
2. Empty one cup of the broth into the burger, but do not stir.
3. Stir in the tomato sauce and paste—but do not stir.
4. Close the top and use the manual high-pressure setting for 10 minutes. When done, natural release, the pressure for 10 minutes; then quick release. Stir and serve.

Texas Chili

Prep & Cook Time: 30 min.

Yields: 4 Servings
Nutrition Values: Calories: 395 | Fat: 24 g | Protein: 30 g | Net Carbs: 9 g

Ingredients:

1 c. chopped onion
1 tbsp. of each:

- Oil
- Minced garlic

1 lb. ground beef
1 c. fire-roasted diced tomatoes—canned okay
1 tbsp. chopped chipotle chilies in adobo sauce—canned
½ c. water
2 corn tortillas

Spice Mixture

Ingredients:

1 t. dried oregano
2 t. of each:

- Salt
- Ground cumin

3 t. Mexican red chili powder—not Cayenne

Preparation Method:

1. Use the Instant Pot—sauté function—to warm the oil. Toss the garlic and onions—stirring for approximately 30 seconds. Blend in the beef as you break it apart.
2. Stir the chipotle chili, canned tomatoes, and tortillas until smooth.
3. Combine the spices in a small dish. Add to the beef and simmer for about 30 seconds. Stir in the tortilla mixture and tomatoes. Add about ½ cup of water into the emptied blender and pour it into the Instant Pot.
4. Secure the lid and cook for 10 minutes on high pressure, with a 10-minute natural release. Quick release the rest of the pressure.
5. Stir and top off with some cheese (add the carbs) and serve.

White Chicken Chili

Prep & Cook Time: 25 min.

Yields: 4 Servings
Nutrition Values: Calories: 204 | Fat: 12 g | Protein: 15 g | Net Carbs: 6 g

Ingredients:

2 lb. chicken breasts—skinless—boneless

4 diced celery stalks

2 diced onions

10 minced garlic cloves

1-2 minced jalapeno peppers

1 t. of each:

- Coriander powder
- Cumin
- Oregano

1 tbsp. of each:

- Salt—to taste
- Chili powder

¼ t. freshly cracked black pepper

4 c. chicken broth

1 pkg. frozen (1 lb.) corn

1 can (15 oz.) cannellini beans—rinsed

Ingredients for Serving:

- Cilantro
- Hot Sauce

Preparation Method:

1. Mix everything into the Instant Pot (omit the beans and corn).
2. Secure the lid and set on high pressure for 15 minutes.
3. Quick release the pressure and shred the chicken in the pot, adding the corn and cannellini beans. Sauté for 5 minutes until heated. Serve.

Chapter 3: Keto Beef Choices

These are some tasty dishes you will surely want to add to your next dinnertime menu plan.

Balsamic Beef Pot Roast

Prep & Cook Time: 1 hr. 5 min.

Yields: 10 Servings
Nutrition Values: Calories: 393 | Fat: 28 g | Protein: 30 g | Net Carbs: 3 g

Ingredients:

1 t. of each:

- Ground black pepper
- Garlic powder

1 tbsp. kosher salt
1 (3 lb.) boneless chuck roast
¼ c. balsamic vinegar
½ c. chopped onion
2 c. water
¼ t. xanthan gum
For the Garnish: Chopped fresh parsley

Preparation Method:

1. Slice the roast in half and season with the garlic powder, pepper, and salt.
2. Prepare the pot using the sauté function and brown the meat.

3. Pour in the onion, water, and vinegar. Secure the lid and set for 35 minutes. Natural release the pressure in the Instant Pot.
4. Add the meat to a container and break it apart. Discard fat and use the sauté function to simmer the juices in the pot. Add the meat back after whisking in the xanthan gum. Gently stir and turn off the heat.
5. Garnish as desired.

Beef Tips Stroganoff

Prep & Cook Time: 38 min.

Yields: 4 Servings
Nutrition Values: Calories: 321 | Fat: 16 g | Protein: 33 g | Net Carbs: 7 g

Ingredients:

1 tbsp. of each:

- Oil
- Garlic
- Worcestershire sauce

½ c. diced onions
1 lb. beef/pork stew meat
1 ½ c. chopped mushrooms
1 t. salt
½ t. pepper to taste
¾ c. water

Ingredients to Finish:

¼ t. arrowroot starch/cornstarch/xanthan gum
1/3 c. sour cream

Preparation Method:

1. Prepare the Instant Pot using the sauté function. Heat the oil and toss in the garlic and onions. Stir a minute and add the rest of the fixings except for the sour cream.
2. Secure the lid and set on high pressure for 20 minutes. Natural release.
3. Change to the sauté function and stir in the sour cream.

Sprinkle in the xanthan gum slowly, stirring as it thickens.

4. Serve and enjoy with some low-carb noodles or cauliflower rice but add the carbs.

Chipotle Shredded Beef

Prep & Cook Time: 1 hr. 35 min.

Yields: 16 Servings
Nutrition Values: Calories: 334 | Fat: 25.6 g | Protein: 22.6 g | Net Carbs: 2.2 g

Ingredients:

2 tbsp. olive oil
2 t. salt
1 t. black pepper
3 lb. beef chuck roast
1 tbsp. adobo sauce—from chipotle with adobe can
1 chipotle in adobo—seeds removed or not—chopped
2 t. dried of each:

- Oregano
- Cumin

½ t. chili powder
1 c. fresh cilantro—roughly chopped
1 seeded green bell pepper—large chunks
1 peeled – quartered onion
1 c. water.

Preparation Method:

1. Sprinkle the roast with the pepper and salt. Choose the Instant Pot's sauté function and pour in the oil. Arrange the roast in the pot and sauté 3-4 minutes on each side.
2. Spread with the adobo sauce a chipotle pepper. Sprinkle with the chili powder, oregano, and cumin. Toss the cilantro on top. Add the peppers and onions. Pour the water into the pot.

3. Prepare for 60 minutes using the high-pressure setting. Natural release and remove the meat. Shred with two forks and discard the veggies.
4. Add the beef back into the juices. Keep warm until ready to serve.

Greek Meatballs With Tomato Sauce

Prep & Cook Time: 40 min.

Yields: 6 Servings
Nutrition Values: Calories: 261 | Fat: 16 g | Protein: 15 g | Net Carbs: 12 g

Ingredients for the Meatballs:

1 slightly beaten egg
1 lb. ground beef
¼ c. chopped parsley
½ c. finely chopped onion
1/3 c. Arborio rice
To Taste: Pepper and salt

Ingredients for the Sauce:

1 c. water
14 oz. diced tomatoes
½ t. of each:
- Smoked paprika
- Cinnamon

1 t. dried oregano
¼ t. ground cloves
To Taste: More pepper & salt

Preparation Method:

1. Mix all of the meatballs fixings, shaping into eight to ten balls. Arrange in a single layer in the pot.
2. Mix the sauce components in a dish and pour over the prepared meatballs.

3. Program the Instant Pot for 15 minutes under high pressure and release the pressure with the natural release option.
4. Remove the meatballs and blend the sauce until smooth with an immersion blender. Pour over the meatballs, garnish, and serve.

Italian Meatballs

Prep & Cook Time: 35 min.

Yields: 5 Servings
Nutrition Values: Calories: 455 | Fat: 33 g | Protein: 34 g | Net Carbs: 5 g

Ingredients for the Meatballs:

1 ½ lb. ground beef—lean
2 tbsp. freshly chopped parsley
2 eggs
½ c. almond flour
¾ c. grated parmesan cheese
¼ t. of each:

- Garlic Powder
- Ground black pepper
- Dried oregano

1 t. of each:

- Kosher salt
- Dried onion flakes

1/3 c. warm water

Cooking Ingredients:

1 t. olive oil
3 c. keto-friendly marinara sauce/sugar-free sauce

Preparation Method:

1. Mix all of the meatball fixings and shape into 15 (2-inch) balls.
2. Add the oil to the Instant Pot and program the sauté

function. Brown the meatballs by leaving a ½-inch space between each one in the pot. You can also brown them in a skillet first.

3. Pour in the marinara sauce and secure the lid on low pressure for 10 minutes.
4. Natural release the pressure and serve the tasty treat.

Shepherd's Pie

Prep & Cook Time: 45 min.

Yields: 12 Servings
Nutrition Values: Calories: 303 | Fat: 21.2 g | Protein: 21.5 g | Net Carbs: 4.1 g

Ingredients:

1 c. water
4 tbsp. butter
1 head cauliflower
4 oz. cream cheese
1 c. mozzarella
1 egg
Pepper & Salt to taste
1 tbsp. garlic powder
2 lb. ground beef
2 c. of each:

- Frozen peas
- Frozen carrots

8 oz. sliced mushrooms
1 c. beef broth

Preparation Method:

1. Pour the water into the Instant Pot and arrange the cauliflower on top with the leaves and stems removed. Close the lid and set for 5 minutes using high pressure.
2. Quick release and add the cauliflower to a blender. Add the cream cheese, butter, mozzarella, egg, pepper, and salt. Blend until smooth.
3. Drain the water from the Instant Pot. Toss in the beef, carrots,

peas, garlic powder, and broth with a bit more pepper and salt to your liking.

4. Blend in the cauliflower mixture and cook for 10 minutes on high (manual function).
5. Serve and enjoy!

Steak & Cheese Pot Roast

Prep & Cook Time: 1 hr. 15 min.

Yields: 8 Servings
Nutrition Values: Calories: 425 | Fat: 25.7 g | Protein: 46.1 g | Net Carbs: 3.5 g

Ingredients:

1 tbsp. oil
2 large thinly sliced onions
8 oz. sliced mushrooms
1-2 tbsp. Montreal steak seasoning/another favorite Keto choice
1 tbsp. butter
½ c. beef stock
3 lb. chuck roast
Optional: Keto cheese of choice—add the carbs

Preparation Method:

1. Program the Instant Pot to sauté and pour in the oil.
2. Rub the roast with the seasoning. Sauté for 1-2 minutes per side. Remove and add the butter and onions. Toss in the mushrooms, peppers, stock, and roast.
3. Choose the manual high-pressure for 35 minutes and natural release.
4. Shred the meat, sprinkle with cheese, and use as desired.

Chapter 4: Chicken Keto Meals

Bruschetta Chicken

Prep & Cook Time: 1 hr.

Yields: 4 Servings
Nutrition Values: Calories: 480 | Fat: 26 g | Protein: 52 g | Net Carbs: 4 g

Ingredients:

2 tbsp. balsamic vinegar
2 t. minced garlic cloves
1 t. black pepper
½ t. sea salt
1/3 c. olive oil
½ c. sun-dried tomatoes in olive oil
2 lb. chicken breasts—quartered—boneless
2 tbsp. chopped fresh basil

Preparation Method:

1. Whisk the vinegar, oil, garlic, pepper, and salt together. Fold in the tomatoes and basil. Put the breasts in a freezer bag with the mixture for 30 minutes.
2. Add all of the fixings into the Instant Pot and secure the lid.
3. Select the poultry setting (9 minutes). Natural release the pressure for 5 minutes, quick release, and serve.

Creamy Instant Pot Chicken

Prep & Cook Time: 30 min.

Yields: 4 Servings
Nutrition Values: Calories: 405 | Fat: 31 g | Protein: 21 g | Net Carbs: 9 g

Ingredients for the Sauce:

6 garlic cloves
1 chopped onion
1 to 2-inch knots of ginger
½ c. full-fat coconut milk
1 tbsp.—powdered chicken broth base
1 can (10 oz.) Rotel canned tomato and chilis
1 t. ground turmeric

Ingredients for the Chicken:

1 ½ c. chopped celery
2 c. chopped Swiss chard
1 lb. chicken thighs

Ingredient for the Finish:

½ c. full-fat coconut milk

Preparation Method:

1. Put the coconut milk, broth base, turmeric, garlic, onion, ginger, tomatoes, and chilis into a blender. Roughly puree the sauce and add to the Instant Pot.
2. Toss in the celery, chard, and chopped chicken.

3. Select the soup setting (5 minutes, under high pressure). Natural release for 10 minutes, and quick release the rest.
4. Pour in the remainder of the coconut milk, stir, and enjoy.

French Garlic Chicken

Prep & Cook Time: 30 min.

Yields: 4 Servings
Nutrition Values: Calories: 429 | Fat: 37 g | Protein: 19 g | Net Carbs: 4 g

Ingredients for the Marinade:

2 tbsp. olive oil
2 t. Herbes de Provence
1 tbsp. of each:

- Prepared Dijon mustard
- Cider vinegar
- Minced garlic

1 t. of each:

- Pepper
- Salt

1 lb. chicken thighs—no bones or skin

Other Ingredients:

8 chopped garlic cloves
2 tbsp. butter
¼ c. of each:

- Cream
- Water

Preparation Method:

1. Prepare the Marinade: Add all of the fixings using a whisk. Add the chicken and marinate for 30 minutes at

room temperature. (Place in the fridge if it will take longer.)

2. Choose the sauté button and add the butter to melt. Sauté the garlic for 2-3 minutes.
3. Toss in the chicken. Reserve the marinade. Lightly brown the chicken. Pour in the water and marinade into the pot and secure the lid. Cook for 10 minutes and check the temperature. (Internal temperature must be 165°F.)
4. Transfer the chicken to a plate and add the cream to the Instant Pot, mixing well.
5. Serve with the sauce and enjoy.

Lemon Rotisserie Chicken

Prep & Cook Time: 40 min.

Yields: 6 Servings
Nutrition Values: Calories: 284 | Fat: 18.8 g | Protein: 25.7 g | Net Carbs: 2.9 g

Ingredients:

2.5 lb. whole chicken
2 tbsp. olive oil
4 lemon wedges—1 lemon
1 ½ t. salt
1 t. of each:

- Paprika
- Garlic powder

½ t. ground black pepper
1 c. chicken broth

Preparation Method:

1. Wash the chicken and dry it with a paper towel. Insert the lemon wedges into the cavity of the bird.
2. Choose the sauté function in the Instant Pot.
3. Combine the pepper, garlic powder, salt, oil, and paprika in a dish. Rub the top of the chicken (breast side down) using ½ of the spice mixture.
4. Sauté for 3 to 4 minutes.
5. Rub the rest on the other half and flip, cooking 1 more minute.
6. Transfer the chicken to a container and add the trivet to the pot. Put the chicken back (breast side down), and cover with the broth.

7. Secure the lid and set the timer for 20 minutes. Natural release the pressure at the end of the cooking cycle. Serve.

Whole Chicken & Gravy

Prep & Cook Time: 45 min.

Yields: 12 Servings
Nutrition Values: Calories: 450 | Fat: 30.2 g | Protein: 34.5 g |Net Carbs: 0.7 g

Ingredients:

6 ½ lb. whole chicken
2 tbsp. olive oil
½ t. of each:

- Onion powder
- Salt
- Black pepper
- Garlic powder

1 t. dried Italian seasonings
1 ½ c. chicken broth (low-sodium)
2 t. guar gum

Preparation Method:

1. Rub one tablespoon of the oil over the entire chicken, and the rest of the oil into the Instant Pot. Combine the dry seasonings and sprinkle over the entire chicken.
2. Use the sauté function to warm the oil, adding the chicken—breast side down. Let it sauté for 5 minutes, flip, and empty in the chicken broth.
3. Secure the top and set the timer for 40 minutes (manually). When done, simply quick release the pressure.
4. Add the chicken to a bowl and prepare the gravy with the guar gum in the hot broth. Stir until thickened. You can

add another teaspoon if it isn't thick as you like it.
5. Serve with gravy and a sprinkle of chopped parsley.

Chapter 5: Other Tasty Dishes

Whether it is pork, lamb, or another choice; this is one yummy section!

Mutton Curry

Prep & Cook Time: 40 min.

Yields: 4 Servings
Nutrition Values: Calories: 253 | Fat: 13.5 g | Protein: 24.65 g | Net Carbs: 6.34 g

Ingredients:

3 tbsp. oil/ghee
1 lb. mutton bone-in (1-2-inch bits)
1 large (11 oz.) finely chopped onion
Optional: 1 green chili
½ tbsp. minced of each:

- Ginger
- Garlic

1 tbsp. lemon juice
1 med. chopped tomato
Garnish: Cilantro

Spices:

2 t. coriander
1 t. of each:

- Cayenne/red chili powder

- Salt
- Garam masala

¼ t. turmeric

Whole Spices:

6 of each:

- Cloves
- Black peppercorns

½ t. cumin seeds
1 bay leaf
1 (1-inch) cinnamon stick
2 black cardamom

Preparation Method:

1. Use the sauté function in the Instant Pot and pour in the oil. Fold in the whole spices and sauté for 30 seconds. Stir in the onions, green chilies, and garlic. Sauté for 4 minutes.

2. Blend in the spices and chopped tomatoes, stirring for another 2 minutes.

3. Stir in the mutton and mix well, sautéing for another 2 minutes.

4. Close the lid and change to the meat function for 20 minutes.

5. Natural release the pressure and add the lemon juice. Garnish with the mutton curry and cilantro. Enjoy!

Pork

Carnitas

Prep & Cook Time: 1 hr. 16 min.

Yields: 11 Servings
Nutrition Values: Calories: 160 | Fat: 7 g | Protein: 20 g | Net Carbs: 1 g

Ingredients:

2 ½ lb. shoulder blade roast—trimmed and boneless
2 t. kosher salt
Black pepper—to your liking
1 ½ t. cumin
6 minced garlic cloves
½ t. sazon GOYA
¼ t. dry oregano
¾ c. reduced-sodium chicken broth/homemade
2 bay leaves
2-3 chipotle peppers in adobo sauce—to taste
¼ t. dry adobo seasoning—for example, Goya
½ t. garlic powder

Preparation Method:

1. Prepare the roast with pepper and salt. Sear it for about 5 minutes in a skillet.
2. Let it cool and insert the garlic slivers into the roast using a blade (approximately 1-inch deep). Season with the garlic powder, sazon, cumin, oregano, and adobo.
3. Arrange the chicken in the Instant Pot, and add the broth, chipotle peppers, and bay leaves. Stir and secure the lid.

Prepare using high pressure for 50 minutes (meat button).

4. Natural release the pressure and shred the pork. Combine with the juices and discard the bay leaves.
5. Add a bit more cumin and adobo if needed. Stir well and serve.

Chipotle Pork Roast

Prep & Cook Time: 1 hr. 22 min.

Yields: 4 Servings
Nutrition Values: Calories: 460 | Fat: 31 g | Protein: 40 g | Net Carbs: 4 g

Ingredients:

7 ¼ oz. diced tomatoes—canned okay
6 oz. bone broth
2 oz. mild diced canned green chilis
2 lb. pork roast
½ t. of each:

- Cumin
- Onion powder

1 t. chipotle powder

Preparation Method:

1. Combine all of the ingredients in your Instant Pot.
2. Close the top of the pot and use the manual setting for 60 minutes.
3. Do a natural release of the pressure. Serve and enjoy.

Pork Ribs

Prep & Cook Time: 1 hr. 10 min.

Yields: 6 Servings
Nutrition Values: Calories: 387 | Fat: 29 g | Protein: 27 g | Net Carbs: 2 g

Ingredients:

1 pkg. (5 lb.) country style pork ribs

Ingredients for the Rub:

1 tbsp. erythritol/another sweetener
1 t. of each:

- Paprika
- Onion powder
- Garlic powder

½ t. of each:

- Black pepper
- Ground coriander
- Allspice

Ingredients for the Sauce:

2 tbsp. of each:

- Erythritol/your favorite sweetener
- Red wine vinegar

½ c. of each:

- Reduced-sugar/homemade
- Water

¼ c. liquid smoke
½ t. onion powder

½ tbsp.—ground—of each:

- Allspice
- Mustard

¼ t. xanthan gum—optional

Preparation Method:

1. Rub down the ribs with the combined seasonings and stack in the Instant Pot. Mix the sauce fixings and pour over the ribs.
2. Secure the lid and set for 35 minutes (manually) under high pressure.
3. Natural release the pressure and place the ribs in a container to keep warm.
4. Whisk in the xanthan gum (if using) and cook the juices for 10 minutes using the sauté function.
5. Serve and enjoy!

Pork Veggies & Noodles

Prep & Cook Time: 20 min.

Yields: 6 Servings
Nutrition Values: Calories: 241 | Fat: 18 g | Protein: 15 g | Net Carbs: 3 g

Ingredients:

1 tbsp. oil
1 lb. ground pork
1 c. chopped bell peppers
2 garlic cloves
½ c. chopped onion
4 c. chopped baby spinach
2 pkg. shirataki noodles
½ c. grated parmesan cheese

Preparation Method:

1. Prepare the Instant Pot on the sauté function and add the oil when hot.
2. Toss in the pork and sauté until slightly pink. Add the garlic, onions, peppers, and spinach. Scrape the browning bits from the bottom and secure the lid.
3. Use the high-pressure setting for 3 minutes and quick release the pressure. Empty the sauce over the noodles and garnish with the cheese.

Spicy Pork—Korean Style

Prep & Cook Time: 40 min.

Yields: 4 Servings
Nutrition Values: Calories: 189 | Fat: 10 g | Protein: 15 g | Net Carbs: 9 g

Ingredients:

1 lb. pork shoulder
1 thinly sliced onion
1 tbsp. of each:

- Minced garlic
- Minced ginger
- Soy sauce
- Sesame oil
- Rice wine

2 Splenda packs
1 t. Cayenne
2 tbsp. Gochugaru Chili flakes
¼ c. water

Ingredients for Finishing:

¼ c. sliced green onion
1 tbsp. sesame seeds
1 thinly sliced onion

Preparation Method:

1. Cut the pork into ¼- to ½-inch slices and add the rest of the marinade ingredients into a container. Let this rest for 1 hour to 24 hours. When ready to cook, use the high-

pressure setting for 20 minutes. Natural release.

2. Use a cast iron skillet to cook the thinly sliced onion and pork cubes. Once the pan is hot, just empty in the sauce, and mix with the pork.
3. When the sauce has cooled down, the onions will be soft. Toss the green onions and sesame seeds and serve.

Chapter 6: Desserts

These are so delicious that you may forget they are ketogenic!

Chocolate Blueberry Cake

Prep & Cook Time: 20 min.

Yields: 8 Servings
Nutrition Values: Calories: 164 | Fat: 9.2 g | Protein: 3.2 g | Net Carbs: 4 g

Ingredients:

1 t. unsweetened chocolate—melted
½ c. favorite sugar substitute
1 pinch—salt
½ t. baking powder
1 tbsp. heavy cream
1 c. almond flour
½ c. of each:

- Almond milk
- Blueberries

Preparation Method:

1. Combine your chosen sugar substitute and the melted chocolate in a mixing container. Stir in the cream and almond milk, gently blending.

2. Mix well and add the berries.

3. Prepare a cake pan and place in the Instant Pot on a trivet. Add 1 cup of water to the pot and close the lid.
4. Cook using the medium pressure setting (8 minutes).
5. Natural release the pressure and serve as it is or chilled.

Chocolate Mini Cakes

Prep & Cook Time: 15 min.

Yields: 2 Servings
Nutrition Values: Calories: 193 | Fat: 12 g | Protein: 15 g | Net Carbs: 9 g

Ingredients:

2 large eggs

2 tbsp. each of:

- Splenda/your favorite sweetener
- Heavy cream

½ t. baking powder

¼ c. baking cocoa

1 t. vanilla extract

Preparation Method:

1. Add one cup of water and the trivet to the Instant Pot.
2. Combine all of the dry ingredients and mix well.
3. Mix in another dish and blend in the rest of the ingredients (eggs, cream, and vanilla extract).

4. Spray the ramekins and fill each one halfway. Carefully add them to the cooker and secure the lid.
5. Prepare for 9 minutes using the high-pressure setting.
6. Quick release the pressure and add to a plate to cool.

Coconut Cake

Prep & Cook Time: 50 min.

Yields: 8 Servings
Nutrition Values: Calories: 236 | Fat: 23 g | Protein: 5 g | Net Carbs: 3 g

Dry Ingredients:

1 c. almond flour
½ c. unsweetened shredded coconut
1/3 c. Truvia
1 t. of each:

- Apple pie spice
- Baking powder

Wet Ingredients:

¼ c. melted butter
2 lightly whisked eggs
½ c. heavy whipping cream

Also Needed:

- 1 (6-inch) round cake pan
- 2 c. water

Preparation Method:

1. Combine all of the dry fixings. Add each of the "wet" ingredients—one at a time. Empty the batter into the pan, and cover with foil.

2. Empty the water into the Instant Pot and place the steamer rack.
3. Set the timer for 40 minutes using the high-pressure setting. Natural release for 10 minutes. Then, quick release.
4. Remove the pan and let it cool for 15 to 20 minutes. Flip it over onto a platter and garnish as desired (count the carbs).

Orange Rum Cake

Prep & Cook Time: 20 min.

Yields: 8 Servings
Nutrition Values: Calories: 262 | Fat: 22 g | Protein: 7 g | Net Carbs: 4 g

Ingredients:

3 eggs
2 t. baking powder
1 ½ c. almond flour
½ c. of each:

- Butter—softened
- Coconut flour

1 t. each of orange:

- Extract
- Zest

¼ t. xanthan gum
1 pinch—salt
¾ c. granulated erythritol sweetener
1 c. almond milk
3 tbsp. gold rum

Preparation Method:

1. Combine in a blender: Eggs, zest, orange extract, gold rum, almond milk, erythritol, and the butter.
2. Blend for 1 minute and add the rest of the fixings (baking powder, almond flour, xanthan gum, coconut flour, and salt). Blend for an additional 20 seconds.
3. Grease a pan to fit inside the Instant Pot on the trivet. Pour in 1 cup of water and secure the lid.

4. Use the high-pressure setting (8 minutes).
5. Quick release the pressure and let it cool for about 10 minutes before serving.

Ricotta Lemon Cheesecake

Prep & Cook Time: 50 min.

Yields: 6 Servings
Nutrition Values: 181 Calories | Fat: 16 g | Protein: 5 g | Net Carbs: 2 g

Ingredients:

8 oz. cream cheese
¼ c. Truvia
1 lemon—Zest and juice
1/3 c. Ricotta cheese
½ t. lemon extract
2 eggs

Ingredients for the Topping:

1 t. Truvia
2 tbsp. sour cream

Also Needed:

1 (6-inch) springform pan

Preparation Method:

1. Combine all of the fixings in a stand mixer (Omit the eggs for now.).
2. Taste test and add the eggs. Use the low speed since overbeating the eggs will cause the crust to crack.
3. Add the batter to the pan. Cover with foil/silicone lid.
4. Add the trivet and two cups of water and arrange the pan

in the Instant Pot.

5. Cook for 30 minutes (high-pressure). Natural release the pressure.
6. Blend in the Truvia and sour cream. Decorate the warm cake and place in the fridge to chill for 6 to 8 hours.

Conclusion

Thanks again for taking the time to download your copy of the *Ketogenic Instant Pot Cookbook*! You will discover all of the reasons you will enjoy these delicious recipes once you know how convenient and energy efficient meal planning is when you own an Instant Pot.

The meal combinations are flexible, and you will soon discover what you have been missing out of life with so much less time consumed in food prep. You know this will be a great addition to your cookbook resources. It will surely be frequently used as you plan your weekly meal plans.

You now see how easy it can be to measure out the ingredients and follow the step-by-step information provided for each of the tasty recipes. All you need to do is gather a shopping list of what you need to become ketogenic and heat to the superstore for supplies.

Enjoy!

Index for the Recipes

Chapter 1: Delicious Breakfast Choices

Chapter 2: Luncheon Dishes

Soups

Chilis & Stews

Chicken Stew
Lamb Stew
No-Beans Beef Chili
Texas Chili
White Chicken Chili

Chapter 3: Keto Beef Choices

Balsamic Beef Pot Roast
Beef Tips Stroganoff
Chipotle Shredded Beef
Greek Meatballs with Tomato Sauce
Italian Meatballs
Shepherd's Pie
Steak & Cheese Pot Roast

Chapter 4: Keto Chicken Meals

Bruschetta Chicken
Creamy Instant Pot Chicken
French Garlic Chicken
Lemon Rotisserie Chicken
Whole Chicken & Gravy

Chapter 5: Other Tasty Dishes

Mutton Curry

Pork

Chapter 6: Desserts—Snacks & Appetizers

Description

You will be surprised how many tasty recipes are waiting for your approval in your copy of the *Ketogenic Instant Pot Cookbook: Make Yummy Ketogenic Diet Meals with Instant Pot*. You can use these tasty recipes if you want to maintain a healthy ketogenic diet, lose weight, and still enjoy delicious food items.

Planning your meals in advance will become much less trouble with the delicious meals downloaded to your files. Each of these recipes is focused on the Instant Pot using ketogenic-friendly diet foods.

These are just a few of the delicious choices to make your kitchen time limited:

- Sausage Cheese Ring
- Lamb Stew
- Paprika Boiled Eggs
- French Garlic Chicken
- Orange Rum Cake

You will discover many ways to use your Instant Pot for breakfast, lunch, and dinner. The Instant Pot will save you many hours of preparation time, so you can move on with your life and get out of the kitchen.

Enjoy your new cooking experience; starting right now!

Ketogenic Recipes

Make Satisfying Tasty Ketogenic Meals

Table of Contents

presented is without assurance regarding its continued validity or interim quality. Trademarks that mentioned are done without written consent and can in no way be considered an endorsement from the trademark holder.

Introduction

Congratulations on acquiring your personal copy of the *Ketogenic Recipes: Make Satisfying Tasty Ketogenic Meals.* I am so excited that you have chosen to take a new path using the Ketogenic diet plan. The plan is recognized by several names including the low-carb diet, Ketogenic low-carbohydrate diet & high-fat (LCHF) diet plan, and the Keto diet.

Your liver produces ketones which are used as energy to provide sufficient levels of protein. The process of ketosis is natural and occurs daily – no matter the total of carbs consumed. Before you begin the journey to ketosis; here is a bit of insight on how the diet plan was discovered:

During the course of history as early as the 20th century, fasting was theorized by Bernard McFadden/Bernarr Macfadden as a means for restoring your health. One of his students introduced a treatment for epilepsy using the same plan. In 1912, it was reported by the *New York Medical Journal* that the fast is a successful method to treat epileptic patients, followed by a starch- and sugar-free diet.

In 1921, Rollin Woodyatt noted the ketone bodies (three water-soluble compounds, β-hydroxybutyrate, acetone, and acetoacetate) were produced by the liver as a result of a diet low in carbohydrates and rich in fat.

Also, in 1921, Dr. Russell Wilder who worked for the Mayo Clinic became well-known when he formulated the keto plan which was then used as part of the epilepsy therapy treatment plan. He had a huge interest in the plan because he also suffered from epilepsy. The plan became known for its other effects which helped in weight loss, and many other ailments.

The ketosis dieting technique was set aside in the 1940s because "improved" methods were discovered for the treatment of epilepsy. However, during that time - approximately 30% of the cases using the alternate plan failed. Therefore, the original ketogenic plan was reintroduced to the patients. As of 2016, Wilder is still functioning successfully without the seizure episodes.

As a direct result of Dr. Wilder's discovery, innovation began at the Mayo Clinic. Another physician standardized the diet plan using the following calculation:

- 10-15 carbs daily
- 1 gram of protein per kilogram of bodyweight
- The remainder of the count will remain with fat

As time passed, the plan had a few changes to make it functional as it is today.

The Charlie Foundation was founded by the family of Charlie Abraham in 1994 after his recovery from seizures he had daily, and other health issues. Charlie—as a youngster—was placed on the diet and continued to use it for five years. As of 2016, he is still functioning successfully without the seizure episodes and is furthering his education as a college student.

The Charlie Foundation appointed a panel of dietitians and neurologists to form an agreement in the form of a statement in 2006. It was written as an approval of the diet and stated which cases its use would be considered. It is noted that the plan is especially recommended for children.

Now, it is time for you to enjoy the same plan!

Chapter 1: Lunchtime Favorites

Salads

Bistro Steak Salad with Horseradish Dressing

Serves: 2

Nutritional Values Per Serving:

Calories: 736 | Protein: 41.4 g | Carbohydrates: 6.2 g| Fat: 59.4 g

Ingredients:

- 1 (12 oz.) rib-eye steak
- ¼ t. of each:
- -Pepper
- -Salt
- 1 (2.1 oz.) small red onion
- 1 (7 oz.) bag romaine salad greens
- 4 slices uncured bacon
- ½ cup (2 oz.) sliced radishes
- 4.2 oz. cherry tomatoes

Ingredients for the Dressing:

- 2 tbsp. prepared horseradish

- ¼ c. mayonnaise (see recipe below)
- Pepper and salt

Method:

1. Thinly slice the onion and radishes.
2. Place parchment paper on a baking tin. Set the oven temperature to 350°F. Arrange the bacon in a single layer in the pan. Bake for 15 minutes. Drain and break into small pieces.
3. Pat the steak with paper towels. Season with the pepper and salt. Grill for four minutes and flip. Continue cooking another 12-15 minutes (medium is approximately 12 minutes or internal temperature of 155°F.).
4. Let it cool down five minutes, and slice against the grain into small slices.
5. Prepare the dressing (below) and enjoy.

Low-Carb Mayonnaise for the Horseradish Dressing

Serves: 4

Nutritional Values Per Serving: Included with above recipe

Ingredients:

- 1 egg yolk
- 1-2 t. white vinegar/lemon juice
- 1 tbsp. Dijon mustard

- 1 c. light olive oil

Method:

1. Ahead of time, take out the egg and mustard to become room temperature.
2. Mix the mustard and egg. Slowly, pour the oil until the mixture thickens.
3. Pour in the lemon juice/vinegar. Stir well. Add a pinch of salt and pepper for additional flavoring.

Caprese Salad

Serves: 4

Nutritional Values Per Serving:

Calories: 190.75 |63.49 g Fat |Carbohydrates: 4.58 g | Protein: 7.71 g

Ingredients:

- 3 c. grape tomatoes
- 4 peeled garlic cloves
- 2 tbsp. avocado oil
- 10 pearl-sized mozzarella balls
- 4 c. baby spinach leaves
- 1/4 c. fresh basil leaves

- 1 tbsp. of each:
- -Brine reserved from the cheese
- -Pesto

Method:

1. Use aluminum foil to cover a baking tray. Program the oven to 400°F. Arrange the cloves and tomatoes on the baking pan and drizzle with the oil.
2. Bake 20-30 minutes until the tops are slightly browned.
3. Drain the liquid (saving one tablespoon) from the mozzarella. Mix the pesto with the brine.
4. Arrange the spinach in a large serving bowl. Transfer the tomatoes to the dish along with the roasted garlic. Drizzle with the pesto sauce.
5. Garnish with the mozzarella balls, and freshly torn basil leaves.

Egg Salad Stuffed Avocado

Serves: 6

Nutritional Values Per Serving:

Calories: 280.57 | Fat: 24.83 g| Carbohydrates: 3.03 g| Protein: 8.32 g

Ingredients:

- 6 large hard-boiled eggs

- 3 celery ribs
- 1/3 med. red onion
- 4 tbsp. mayonnaise
- 2 tbsp. fresh lime juice
- 2 t. brown mustard
- Pepper & salt to taste
- ½ t. cumin
- 1 t. hot sauce
- 3 med. avocados

Method:

1. Begin by chopping the onions, celery, and eggs. Discard the pit and slice the avocado in half.
2. Combine with all of the other fixings except for the avocado.
3. Scoop the salad into the avocado and serve!

Thai Pork Salad

Serves: 2

Nutritional Values Per Serving:

Calories: 461 | Fat: 32.6 g| Carbohydrates: 5.2 g| Protein: 29.2 g

Ingredients for the Salad:

- 2 c. romaine lettuce
- 10 oz. pulled pork
- ¼ medium chopped red bell pepper
- ¼ c. chopped cilantro

Ingredients for the Sauce:

- 2 tbsp. of each:
- -Tomato paste
- -Chopped cilantro
- Juice & zest of 1 lime
- 2 tbsp. (+) 2 t. soy sauce
- 1 t. of each:
- -Red curry paste
- -Five Spice
- -Fish sauce
- ¼ t. red pepper flakes
- 1 tbsp. (+) 1 t. rice wine vinegar
- ½ t. mango extract
- 10 drops liquid stevia

Method:

1. Zest half of the lime and chop the cilantro.
2. Mix all of the sauce fixings.
3. Blend the barbecue sauce components and set aside.
4. Pull the pork apart and make the salad. Pour a glaze over the pork with a bit of the sauce.

Vegetarian Club Salad

Serves: 3

Nutritional Values Per Serving:

Calories: 329.67| Fat: 26.32 g| Carbohydrates: 4.83 g| Protein: 16.82 g

Ingredients:

- 2 tbsp. of each:
- -Mayonnaise
- -Sour cream
- ½ t. of each:
- -Onion powder
- -Garlic powder
- 1 tbsp. milk
- 1 t. dried parsley
- 3 large hard-boiled eggs
- 4 oz. cheddar cheese
- ½ c. cherry tomatoes
- 1 c diced cucumber
- 3 c. torn romaine lettuce
- 1 tbsp. Dijon mustard

Method:

1. Slice the hard-boiled eggs and cube the cheese. Cut the tomatoes into halves and dice the cucumber.
2. Prepare the dressing (dried herbs, mayo, and sour cream) mixing well.
3. Add one tablespoon of milk to the mixture - and another if it's too thick.
4. Layer the salad with the vegetables, cheese, and egg slices. Scoop a spoonful of mustard in the center along with a drizzle of dressing.
5. Toss and enjoy!

Pasta

Cauliflower 'Mac N Cheese'

Serves: 4

Nutritional Values Per Serving:

Calories: 294 | Fat: 23 g| Carbohydrates: 7 g| Protein: 11 g

Ingredients:

- 3 tbsp. butter
- 1 head cauliflower
- 1 c. cheddar cheese
- Black pepper & sea salt to taste
- ¼ c. of each:
- -Unsweetened almond milk
- -Heavy cream

Method:

1. Cut the cauliflower into small florets and shred the cheese.
2. Prepare the oven to 450°F. Cover a baking sheet with aluminum foil or parchment paper.
3. Melt 2 tbsp. of butter. Toss the florets and butter. Give it a shake of pepper and salt. Place the cauliflower on the baking pan and roast 10-15 minutes.
4. Warm up the rest of the butter, milk, heavy cream, and cheese in the microwave or double boiler. Pour on the cheese and serve.

Fettuccine Chicken Alfredo

Serves: 2

Nutritional Values Per Serving:

Calories: 585 | Fat: 51 g| Carbohydrates: 1 g| Protein: 25 g

Ingredients:

- 2 tbsp. butter
- 2 minced garlic cloves
- 1/2 t. dried basil
- 1/2 c. heavy cream
- 4 tbsp. grated parmesan

Ingredients for the Chicken and Noodles:

- 2 chicken thighs - no bones or skin
- 1 tbsp. olive oil

- 1 bag Miracle Noodle - Fettuccini
- Salt and pepper

Method:

1. For the Sauce: Add the cloves to a pan with the butter for two minutes. Empty the cream into the skillet and let it simmer two additional minutes. Toss in one tablespoon of the parmesan at a time. Add the pepper, salt, and dried basil. Simmer three to five minutes on the low heat setting.
2. For the Chicken: Pound the chicken with a meat tenderizer hammer until it is approximately ½-inch thick. Warm up the oil in a skillet using the medium heat setting and put the chicken in to cook for about seven minutes per side. Shred and set aside.
3. For the Noodles: Prepare the package of noodles. Rinse, and boil them for two minutes in a pot of water.
4. Fold in the noodles along with the sauce and shredded chicken. Cook slowly for two minutes and enjoy.

Lemon Garlic Shrimp Pasta

Serves: 4

Nutritional Values Per Serving:

Calories: 360| Fat: 21 g| Carbohydrates: 3.5 g| Protein: 36 g

Ingredients:

- 2 bags angel hair pasta

- 4 garlic cloves
- 2 tbsp. each:
- -Olive oil
- -Butter
- ½ lemon
- 1 lb. large raw shrimp
- ½ t. paprika
- Fresh basil
- Pepper and salt

Method:

1. Drain the water from the package of noodles and rinse them in cold water. Add them to a pot of boiling water for two minutes. Transfer them to a hot skillet over medium heat to remove the excess liquid (dry roast). Set them to the side.
2. Use the same pan to warm the oil, butter, and smashed garlic. Saute a few minutes but don't brown.
3. Slice the lemon into rounds and add them to the garlic along with the shrimp. Saute for approximately three minutes per side.
4. Add the noodles and spices and stir to blend the flavors.

Pizza

BBQ Meat-Lover's Pizza

Serves: 2

Nutritional Values Per Serving:

Calories: 205| Fat: 27 g| Carbohydrates: 3.5 g| Protein: 18 g

Ingredients:

- 2 c. (8 oz.) mozzarella
- 1 tbsp. psyllium husk powder
- ¾ c. almond flour
- 3 tbsp. (1 ½ oz.) cream cheese
- 1 large egg
- ½ t. of each:
- -Black pepper
- -Salt
- 1 tbsp. Italian seasoning

Ingredients for the Topping:

- 1 c. (4 oz.) mozzarella cheese
- To Taste: BBQ sauce
- Sliced Kabana/hard salami
- Bacon slices

- Sprinkled oregano - optional

Method:

1. Set the temperature of the oven to 400°F.
2. Melt the cheese in the microwave until it melts – about 45 seconds. Toss in the cream cheese and egg, mixing well.
3. Blend in the psyllium husk, flour, salt, pepper, and Italian seasoning. Make the dough as circular as possible. Bake for ten minutes. Flip it onto a piece of parchment paper.
4. Cover the crust with the toppings and some more cheese. Bake until the cheese is golden, slice, and serve.

Beef Pizza

Serves: 4

Nutritional Values Per Serving:

Calories: 610| Fat: 45 g |Carbohydrates: 2 g | Protein: 44 g

Ingredients:

- 2 large eggs
- 1 pkg. (20 oz.) ground beef
- 28 pepperoni slices
- ½ c. of each:

- -Shredded cheddar cheese
- -Pizza sauce
- 4 oz. mozzarella cheese
- Also Needed: 1 Cast iron skillet

Method:

1. Combine the eggs, beef, and seasonings. Place in the skillet to form the crust. Bake until the meat is done or about 15 minutes.
2. Take it out and add the sauce, cheese, and toppings. Place the pizza in the

   oven a few minutes until the cheese has melted. Remove and enjoy!

Bell Pepper Basil Pizza

Servings: 4 - 2 Pizzas

Nutritional values per serving:

Calories: 411.5| Fat: 31.32 g| Carbohydrates: 6.46 g| Protein: 22.26 g

Ingredients for the Pizza Base:

- 6 oz. mozzarella cheese
- 2 tbsp. of each:
- -Fresh parmesan cheese

- -Cream cheese
- -Psyllium Husk
- 1 t. Italian seasoning
- 1 large egg
- ½ t. of each:
- -Black pepper
- -Salt

Ingredients for the Toppings:

- 4 oz. shredded cheddar cheese
- ¼ c. marinara sauce
- 1 med. vine ripened tomato
- 2-3 med. bell peppers
- 2-3 tbsp. fresh basil – chopped

Method:

1. Set the temperature in the oven to 400°F.
2. Melt the cheese in the microwave until melted and pliable or for 40-50 seconds. Add the remainder of the pizza base fixings to the cheese – mixing well with your hands.
3. Flatten the dough to form the two circular pizzas. Bake ten minutes. Remove and add the toppings. Take for about 8-10 additional minutes.
4. Let it cool and serve.

Pita Pizza

Serves: 2

Nutritional Values Per Serving:

Calories: 250| Fat: 19 g| Carbohydrates: 4 g| Protein: 13 g

Ingredients:

- ½ c. marinara sauce
- 1 low-carb pita
- 2 oz. cheddar cheese
- 14 slices pepperoni
- 1 oz. roasted red peppers

Method:

1. Set the oven to 450°F.
2. Slice the pita in half and put on a foil-lined baking tray. Rub with a bit of oil and toast for one to two minutes.
3. Pour the sauce over the bread, sprinkle with the cheese, and other toppings. Bake for another five minutes or until the cheese melts.

Tacos & Wraps

Chipotle Fish Tacos

Serves: 4

Nutritional values per serving:

Calories: 300 | Fat: 20 g| Carbohydrates: 7 g| Protein: 24 g

Ingredients:

- ½ small diced yellow onion
- 2 pressed cloves of garlic
- 1 chopped fresh jalapeno
- 2 tbsp. olive oil
- 4 oz. chipotle peppers in adobo sauce
- 2 tbsp. each:
- -Mayonnaise
- -Butter
- 4 low-carb tortillas
- 1 lb. haddock fillets

Method:

1. In a skillet, fry the onion on med-high for five minutes.
2. Lower the temperature to the medium heat setting. Toss in the garlic, and jalapeno. Stir another two minutes.

3. Chop and add the chipotles, along with the adobo sauce into the pan.
4. Drop the butter, mayonnaise, and fish into the pan and cook about eight minutes.
5. Make the Tacos: Fry the tortilla for approximately two minutes for each side. Chill and shape them with the prepared fixings.

Cumin Spiced Beef Wraps

Serves: 2

Nutritional Values Per Serving:

Calories: 375| Fat: 26 g| Carbohydrates: 4 g| Protein: 30 g

Ingredients:

- 1-2 tbsp. coconut oil
- ¼ onion – diced
- 2/3 lb. ground beef
- 2 tbsp. chopped cilantro
- 1 diced red bell pepper
- 1 t. minced ginger
- 2 t. cumin
- 4 minced garlic cloves
- Pepper and salt to your liking

- 8 large cabbage leaves

Method:

1. Warm up a frying pan and pour in the oil. Saute the peppers, onions, and ground beef using medium heat. When done, add the pepper, salt, cumin, ginger, cilantro, and garlic.
2. Fill a large pot with water (3/4 full) and wait for it to boil. Cook each leaf for 20 seconds, plunge it in cold water and drain before placing it on your serving dish.
3. Scoop the mixture onto each leaf, fold, and enjoy.

Chapter 2: Dinnertime Specialties

Beef for Dinner

Balsamic Beef Pot Roast

Serves: 10

Nutritional Values Per Serving:

Calories: 393 | Fat: 28g| Carbohydrates: 3 g| Protein: 30 g

Ingredients:

- 1 boneless (approx. 3 lb.) chuck roast
- 1 t. of each:
- -Garlic powder
- -Black ground pepper
- 1 tbsp. kosher salt
- ¼ c. balsamic vinegar
- ½ c. chopped onion
- 2 c. water
- ¼ t. xanthan gum

For the Garnish:

- Freshly chopped parsley

Method:

1. Combine the salt, garlic powder, and pepper and rub the chuck roast with the combined fixings.
2. Use a heavy skillet to sear the roast. Add the vinegar and deglaze the pan as you continue cooking for one more minute.
3. Toss the onion into a pot with the (two cups) boiling water along with the roast. Cover with a top and simmer for three to four hours on a low setting.
4. Take the meat from the pot and add to a cutting surface. Shred into chunks and remove any fat or bones.
5. Add the xanthan gum to the broth and whisk. Place the roast meat back in the pan to warm up.
6. Serve with a favorite side dish.

Cheeseburger Calzone

Serves: 8

Nutritional Values Per Serving:

Calories: 580| Fat: 47 g| Carbohydrates: 3 g| Protein: 34 g

Ingredients:

- ½ yellow diced onion
- 1 ½ lb. ground beef – lean
- 4 thick-cut bacon strips
- 4 dill pickle spears

- 8 oz. cream cheese – divided
- 1 egg
- ½ c. mayonnaise
- 1 c. of each:
- -Shredded cheddar cheese
- -Almond flour
- -Shredded mozzarella cheese

Method:

1. Program the oven to 425°F. Prepare a cookie tin with parchment paper.
2. Chop the pickles into spears. Set aside for now.
3. Prepare the Crust: Combine ½ of the cream cheese and the mozzarella cheese. Microwave 35 seconds. When it melts, add the egg and almond flour to make the dough. Set aside.
4. Cook the beef on the stove using medium heat.
5. Cook the bacon (microwave for five minutes or stovetop). When cool, break into bits.
6. Dice the onion and add to the beef and cook until softened. Toss in the bacon, cheddar cheese, pickle bits, the rest of the cream cheese, and mayonnaise. Stir well.
7. Roll the dough onto the prepared baking tin. Scoop the mixture into the center. Fold the ends and side to make the calzone.

8. Bake until browned or about 15 minutes. Let it rest for 10 minutes before slicing.

Nacho Steak in the Skillet

Serves: 5

Nutritional Values Per Serving:

Calories: 385.4| Fat: 30.67 g| Carbohydrates: 5.9 g| Protein: 18.87 g

Ingredients:

- 1 tbsp. butter
- 8 oz. beef round tip steak
- 1/3 c. melted refined coconut oil
- ½ t. turmeric
- 1 t. chili powder
- 1 ½ pounds cauliflower
- 1 oz. each shredded:
- -Cheddar cheese
- -Monterey Jack cheese

Possible Garnishes:

- 1 oz. canned jalapeno slices
- 1/3 c. sour cream

- Avocado – Approx. 5 oz.

Method:

1. Set the oven temperature to 400°F.
2. Prepare the cauliflower into chip-like shapes.
3. Combine the turmeric, chili powder, and coconut oil in a mixing dish.
4. Toss in the cauliflower and add it to a tin. Set the baking timer for 20 to 25 minutes.
5. Over med-high heat in a cast iron skillet, add the butter. Cook until both sides are done, flipping just once. Let it rest for five to ten minutes. Thinly slice, and sprinkle with some pepper and salt to the steak.
6. When done, transfer the florets to the skillet and add the steak strips. Top it off with the cheese and bake five to ten more minutes.
7. Serve with your favorite garnish but count those carbs.

Portobello Bun Cheeseburgers

Serves: 6

Nutritional Values Per Serving:

Calories: 336| Fat: 22.8 g| Carbohydrates: 4 g| Protein: 29.1 g

Ingredients:

- 1 lb. ground beef - lean 80/20

- 1 t. of each:
- 1 tbsp. Worcestershire sauce
- -Pink Himalayan salt
- -Ground black pepper
- 1 tbsp. avocado oil
- 6 slices sharp cheddar cheese
- 6 Portobello mushroom caps

Method:

1. Remove the stem, rinse, and dab dry the mushrooms.
2. Combine the salt, pepper, beef, and Worcestershire sauce in a mixing container. Form into patties.
3. Warm up the oil (medium heat). Let the caps simmer about three to four minutes per side.
4. Transfer the mushrooms to a bowl - using the same pan - cook the patties four minutes, flip, and cook another five minutes until done.
5. Add the cheese to the burgers and cover for one minute to melt the cheese.
6. Add one of the mushroom caps to the burgers along with the desired garnishes and serve.

Steak-Lovers Slow-Cooked Chili in the Slow Cooker

Serves: 12

Nutritional Values Per Serving:

Calories: 321| Fat: 26 g| Carbohydrates: 3.3 g| Protein: 38.4 g

With Toppings:
Calories: 540.3| Fat: 41.32 g| Carbohydrates: 13.49 g| Protein: 32.47 g

Ingredients for the Chili:

- 1 c. beef or chicken stock
- ½ c. sliced leeks
- 2 ½ lbs. (1-inch cubes) steak
- 2 c. whole tomatoes (canned with juices)
- 1/8 t. black pepper
- ½ t. salt
- ½ t. cumin
- ¼ t. ground cayenne pepper
- 1 tbsp. chili powder

Optional Toppings:

- 1 t. fresh chopped cilantro
- 2 tbsp. sour cream
- ¼ c/ shredded cheddar cheese
- ½ avocado – sliced or cubed

Method:

1. Toss all of the fixings into the cooker - except the toppings.
2. Use the cooker's high setting for about six hours.
3. Serve, add the toppings, and enjoy.

Vegetarian Keto Burger on a Bun

Serves: 2

Nutritional Values Per Serving:

Calories: 637| Fat: 55.1 g| Carbohydrates: 8.7 g| Protein: 23.7 g

Mushroom Ingredients:

- 1-2 tbsp. freshly chopped basil – 1 t. dried
- 2 medium-large flat mushrooms – ex. Portobello
- 1 tbsp. of each:
- -Coconut oil/ghee
- -Freshly chopped oregano – ½ t. dried
- 1 crushed garlic clove
- ¼ t. salt
- Black pepper

Serving Ingredients:

- 2 large organic eggs
- 2 slices cheddar/gouda cheese
- 2 tbsp. mayonnaise
- 2 keto buns – see recipe below

Also Needed:

1 griddle pan/regular skillet

Method:

1. Prepare the mushrooms for marinating by seasoning with crushed garlic, pepper, salt, ghee (melted), and fresh herbs. Save a small amount for frying the eggs. Marinate for about one hour at room temperature.

2. Arrange the mushrooms in the pan with the top side facing upwards. Cook for about five minutes on the med-high setting. Flip and continue cooking for another five minutes.

3. Remove the pan from the burner and flip the mushrooms over and add the cheese. When it is time to serve, put them under the broiler for a minute or so to melt the cheese.

4. With the remainder of the ghee, fry the eggs leaving the yolk runny. Remove from the heat.

5. Slice the buns and add them to the grill, cooking until crisp for about two to three minutes.

6. To assemble, add one tablespoon of mayonnaise to each bun and top them off with the mushroom, egg, tomato, and lettuce.

7. Put the tops on the buns (see recipe below) and serve.

Keto Buns for the Burger

Serves: 12

Nutritional Values Per Serving:

Calories: 189| Fat: 12.6 g| Carbohydrates: 3.1 g| Protein: 11.6 g

Note: Erythritol has 0.4 g carbohydrates, and Xylitol has 10 g.

Dry Ingredients:

- ½ c. of each:
- -Ground sesame/poppy seeds
- -Flax meal
- -Unflavored whey protein/egg white protein powder
- 1 c. of each:
- -Almond flour
- -Coconut flour
- 1 tbsp. of each:
- -Dried oregano
- -Minced garlic
- -Cream of tartar
- -Xylitol or Erythritol
- 2 tsp. baking soda
- 1 tsp. salt

Wet Ingredients:

- 2 large eggs
- 6 large egg whites
- 1 tbsp. extra-virgin coconut oil
- 2 c. hot water

Method:

1. Prepare the oven temperature to 350°F.
2. Toss the sesame seeds in a processor and pulse until powdery. Blend in all of the dry components, omitting the coconut flour for now. Mix well.
3. Combine the hot water and eggs. Add to the dry fixings, mixing well. Gradually combine the coconut flour until you have a dense uniformity. Be sure not to make the mixture too dry.
4. Scoop the dough onto a baking pan - leaving them several inches apart and sprinkle with the poppy/sesame seeds. Bake for 20-30 minutes or until browned.

Chicken for Dinner

Barbecue Pulled Chicken in the Slow Cooker

Serves: 8

Nutritional Values Per Serving:

Calories: 219| Fat: 7.2 g| Carbohydrates: 4.3 g| Protein: 33.8 g

Ingredients

- 3 lb. chicken thighs
- 1 t. of each:

- -Cumin
- -Smoked paprika
- -Onion powder
- ¼ t. pepper
- ¾ t. salt - divided
- 1 t. maple extract
- ¼ c. apple cider vinegar
- 1 c. sugar-free ketchup
- ½ c. water
- ½ t. clear liquid stevia
- 1 tbsp. unsweetened cocoa powder
- ¼ t. cumin

Method:

1. Remove all of the bones and chicken and arrange the chicken on a baking sheet. Combine the salt, pepper, cumin, onion powder, and paprika together. Rub it over the chicken.
2. Pour the ketchup, vinegar, and water into the slow cooker. Stir, and add the rest of the fixings. Lastly, add the chicken.
3. Close the lid and cook four hours on high or eight hours on low.
4. Enjoy over some rice (add the carbs).

Chicken Parmesan

Serves: 2

Nutritional Values Per Serving:

Calories: 600| Fat: 32 g| Carbohydrates: 3 g| Protein: 74 g

Ingredients:

- 1 lb. breasts of chicken
- 2 tbsp. parmesan cheese
- 1 oz. pork rinds
- 1 egg
- ½ c. of each:
- -Marinara sauce
- -Shredded mozzarella

Possible Garnish Ingredients:

- -Pepper and salt
- -Garlic powder
- -Oregano

Method:

1. Program the oven temperature to 350°F.
2. Use a food processor/Magic Bullet to crush the pork rinds and parmesan cheese. Add them to a bowl.
3. Pound the chicken breasts until they are ½-inch thick. Beat the egg and dip the chicken in for an egg wash. Dip the chicken into the crumbs.
4. Arrange the breasts on a lightly greased baking sheet. Sprinkle with the seasonings and bake 25 minutes.

5. Dump the marinara sauce over each portion. Garnish with the mozzarella and bake for 15 minutes.
6. Enjoy with a bed of spinach.

Coconut Curry Chicken Tenders

Serves: 5

Nutritional Values Per Serving:

Calories: 494 | Fat: 39.4 g| Carbohydrates: 2.1 g| Protein: 29.4 g

Ingredients for the Tenders:

- 1 large egg
- 1 pkg. chicken thighs (24 oz.) deboned with skin /5 thighs
- ½ c. of each:
- -Crumbled pork rinds (1 ½ oz.)
- -Unsweetened shredded coconut
- 1/2 t. coriander
- 2 t. curry powder
- ¼ t. of each:
- -Onion powder
- -Garlic powder
- Pepper & salt to your liking

Sweet and Spicy Mango Dipping Sauce Ingredients:

- ¼ c. of each:
- -Sour cream
- -Mayonnaise
- 1 ½ t. mango extract
- 2 tbsp. sugar-free ketchup
- ¼ t. cayenne pepper
- ½ t. of each:
- -Ground ginger
- -Garlic powder
- -Red pepper flakes
- 7 drops liquid stevia

Method:

1. Set the oven to 400°F.
2. Whisk the eggs and debone the thighs. Slice them into strips (skins on).
3. Add the spices, coconut, and pork rinds to a Ziploc-type bag. Add the chicken, shake, and place on a wire rack. Bake for about 15 minutes. Flip them over and continue baking for another 20 minutes.
4. Combine the sauce components and stir well. Serve with your piping hot chicken tenders

Pizza Chicken Casserole in the Slow Cooker

Serves: 3

Nutritional Values Per Serving:

Calories: 228 | Fat: 8.8 g| Carbohydrates: 6 g| Protein: 31.2 g

Ingredients:

- 2 cubed chicken breasts
- 1 can tomato sauce – 8 oz.
- 1 t. Italian seasoning
- 1 bay leaf
- Dash of pepper
- ¼ t. salt
- To Garnish: ½ c. shredded mozzarella cheese
- Recommended: 2-quart slow cooker

Method:

1. Remove the bones from the chicken and chop into cubes. Add them to the slow cooker.
2. Pour in the sauce over the chicken and add the spices. Stir and cook on the low setting for three to four hours.

Serve with the cheese as a garnish.

Conclusion

Thanks for reading your entire copy of *Ketogenic Recipes: Make Satisfying Tasty Ketogenic Meals*. Let's hope it was informative and provided you with all of the tools you need to achieve your goals of preparing meals on the go that are so nutritious for you and your family.
*
Next, gather all of the new recipes you want to prepare for several days and head to the market. The recipes have provided you with all of the essential nutritional facts so you can prepare a healthy and satisfying meal for you and your active family.

Stay determined by your goals during your transition to ketosis. Follow the instructions and recipe methods. Before long, you will be dropping pounds while enjoying your favorite foods.

Finally, if you found this book useful in any way, a review on Amazon is always appreciated!

Index for the Recipes

Chapter 1: Lunchtime Salads

Salads

Pasta Dishes

Pizza

30668109R00079

Made in the USA
Columbia, SC
29 October 2018